BPO & REO SIMPLIFIED

HOW TO WORK WITH ASSET MANAGERS

BY JAMES A. BROWNING

Copyright © 2011 by James A. Browning

ISBN 0-7414-6493-4

Printed in the United States of America

This is a work of fiction. Names, characters, places, and incidents either are the product of the author's imagination or are used fictitiously. Any resemblance to actual events or locales or persons, living or dead, is entirely coincidental.

Published August 2011

INFINITY PUBLISHING
1094 New DeHaven Street, Suite 100
West Conshohocken, PA 19428-2713
Toll-free (877) BUY BOOK
Local Phone (610) 941-9999
Fax (610) 941-9959
Info@buybooksontheweb.com
www.buybooksontheweb.com

DEDICATION

This book is dedicated to the many special people in my life. First and foremost, to my best friend, love, and partner in life, my wife, Barbara who made this book possible. Next to my sons and daughter, each who are very special to me; Kyle, my oldest son, who is talented, a natural born leader and loving, Jacob, my youngest son, who is compassionate, has wisdom beyond what he knows, and has a heart of platinum, and Amber, my daughter, who brings me more joy today than I could have ever imagined, and has given me the gift of grandchildren. I share this book in spirit with my father, (Josiah) who taught me quietly to be myself & appreciate my family. Finally, to Trish Truax, whose contributions on this book are very much appreciated, and is like a daughter to me!

INCOME=BPO SIMPLIFIED

PRESENTED BY JAMES A. BROWNING
MRE,CEC,FSP,SFR,REO CERTIFIED, SHORT SALE CERTIFIED

Masters in Real Estate, Certified Commercial Education, Broker/Owner Browning Group LLC, Liquidated 115+M REO Properties/last 3 years, 26 years of Commercial Real Estate Experience, Commercial Director for CB NRT-17 years, National Trainer/CREOBA, CEO/The REO Institute of Colorado

Class Overview

The foundation of REO (Real Estate Owned) is the BPO Process (Broker Price Opinion). The first step is understanding what is the purpose of a BPO, who uses it, why and when. The next step is the perfecting of the BPO process; without this process there will not be repeat business. To be a qualified BPO professional, one must always be concise, accurate, and complete the BPO in its entirety.

Learning Objective

- Learn the terminology used by the lenders, banks, and outsourcers.
- Comprehend how to perform a BPO (Broker Price Opinion) on residential properties, or REOs.
- Understand the basics of a BPO.
- Appreciate what the banks/outsourcers need to know about REO properties, and the conditions for performing BPOs.
- We will first define the material, and then work thru an adjustment worksheet.

Why do BPOs?

- Receive more income
- Increase your skills as a Real Estate Professional
- Become more proficient
- Daily business marketing
- Listing opportunities
- Performing BPOs makes you a superior Real Estate Professional

By completing BPOs you can sharpen your skills, and call yourself an expert in:

- Pricing properties
- Placing value on amenities and features
- Inspecting interior/exterior assets and neighborhoods
- Knowing your service area
- Utilizing the MLS and Public Records more efficiently
- Staying current with your local economy and market

What is a BPO?

BPO=Broker Price Opinion, also known as an automated valuation model or detailed market analysis. This is a method used to estimate the probable selling price of a real estate asset. The estimate of price is submitted via computer (AVM) in a BPO report (2-4 pages). This report includes local and regional market conditions, neighborhood analysis, subject property condition, repairs needed, as well as list/sold comparable properties that compare to the subject/asset being priced. This method of estimating a price for the asset has similarities to a Comparable Market Analysis – CMA. These BPOs are specifically assigned to a broker from an outsourcer, lender, or BPO company.

What is an Outsourcer or BPO Company?

This is either a division of a financial institution or a stand alone company. They are also considered to be the "Client". The outsourcer is essentially a middle man between the broker and the banks/lenders. The outsourcer assigns the BPO to the broker, then tracks, expedites, and provides quality assurance/oversight for submitted BPOs. After insuring BPO accuracy, they will then submit to the banks/lenders. The BPO Company is responsible for qualifying and maintaining a list of real estate brokers. There are numerous types of BPO companies. Many only handle BPOs for their clients and these never become listings. Others assign BPOs which may turn into listings. When getting started, it is advisable to register with as many companies as possible. You want to gain as much experience as possible.

Who can perform BPOs?

Realtors, brokers, appraisers (acting in an agent capacity), and active licensees. If you are considering performing BPOs, this must first be discussed with your employing broker and/or attorney to determine the ramifications of performing BPOs in your specific state or market area.

What purpose does a BPO serve, and when is it requested?

The broker is requested to submit a BPO on an asset for a fee. BPOs are requested for foreclosures, REOs, short sales, HELOC's, and due diligence for investors or investment bankers. This request could be made from the 1st stage of delinquency, or for any other reason. For example, if a lender/financial institution needs to make a financial decision on an asset for a refinance, they may request a BPO. The initial request is most often for an exterior BPO.

What is the difference between an Interior and an Exterior BPO?

The first requested BPO is usually an exterior request. This will require an exterior examination of the property, with photo documentation of all exterior details. You will need to make notes on condition, and visible amenities. An exterior BPO takes less time to do than an interior BPO. An interior BPO is requested when the broker is able to access the home, for determination of value for a short sale or refinance, or once the property has become a REO. There are different fees paid for the types of BPOs and different photo requirements. These will be discussed later.

BPO Process

Market Conditions

Comparable Selection should always be based on market conditions. Learning your market areas and understanding the difference between distressed markets vs. normal markets is imperative. Comparables used should reflect the prevailing forces that are driving the same market in which the subject is located. In cases where distressed sales are driving the market, a comment is required that addresses and explains the distressed condition of the market.

Distressed Market: The term distressed comparable indicates a short sale or REO transaction. If the subject is distressed, the property is in pre-foreclosure, foreclosure, is a candidate for short sale in foreclosure, or a REO. Comments must indicate that the market is driven by distressed properties/assets. If a fair market price evaluation is requested and the subject is located in a distressed driven market, distressed comparables must be used. Comments are required indicating the comparables used are distressed due to current market conditions. Adjustments are not needed to account for distressed comparables. Due to potential falling values in a distressed market, it is recommended you use sold comps no more than 3 months old if possible.

If the BPO form does not specify the type of comparable, (arms length transaction, REO, short sales etc.) provide a comment that appropriately labels the comparable. Always read the instructions provided as to types of comparables to use, as these instructions could override common practice.

Normal Market: Short sales, REOs, foreclosures and distressed properties do not exist or are possibly few and far between. Arms length transactions are to be used under normal market conditions. Sold comparables that are not arm's length transactions should only be used if no other comps are available. Comments are required for each comparable that is not an arms length transaction. Take extra care in evaluating the comparables and value adjustments should be made to account for the fact that a comparable is not an arm's length transaction. The standard of using sold comps up to 6 months old applies.

Stable Market: There is an equal amount of supply (assets) and demand (buyers). Sold comparables should be no more than 6 months old. A stable market exists when no more than 3% appreciation or depreciation has occurred in the last 6 months. A comment is required if the comparable is over 6 months old. Comps older than 6 months should not be used unless there are limited comps from which to choose.

Rapid Market: There is an abundance of buyers, with a short supply of product/inventory. In this type of market, sold comparables should be no more than 3 months old. A rapid market exists when there is more than 3% appreciation or depreciation in the last 6 months. Comments are required if a rapid market exists. Comments are also required if comparables are over 3 months old.

Lack of Comparables: This is a scenario where there is a short supply of inventory. If comparables are not immediately available, expand search parameters one at a time, starting with the least impact on value. Please note that values will differ from market to market. The following are common criteria that can be expanded: concessions, lot size, year of construction, square footage, room count, date of sale, and proximity.

Preparing to complete the BPO

After you receive confirmation to complete a BPO, and prior to visiting the property, you must gather information on your subject including Property Profile and Assessor Records, Deed Records and MLS print outs on the subject.

You will be required to input specific property information often including: parcel # (PIN), official style, age, square footage, bedrooms, baths, basement size, number of rooms in basement, lot size, annual taxes, delinquent taxes, HOA information, lender, date of last sale and sales price, current list price (if currently on market), and days on market.

Visiting the Property

Always follow specific instructions from the BPO company. For an initial drive by or exterior BPO, DO NOT contact the owner/seller/tenant unless requested by the outsourcer. DO NOT make assumptions regarding interior condition, features, or needed interior repairs. For an interior BPO, you may be directed to contact the listing agent, if the property is listed, or the present owner to gain entry.

Many BPO companies will have a cheat sheet for you to print out and take with you to the property to complete. This will make your data entry easier. Otherwise, plan to take detailed notes on both the exterior/interior condition, as applicable. Always include in your notes information on type of flooring, countertops, appliances, walls, basement, baths, bedrooms, all other rooms, windows, decks, patios, mechanical systems, etc.

The Selection of Comparables

The selection of comparables is one of the most important steps in completing a BPO. Your final determination of value will be directly related to the comparables selected. In addition to the comps selected, you should run a summary of solds, actives, and pending comps in the subject's subarea to determine number of sales, listings, as well as lowest, average, and high list and sold prices.

a) The BPO typically consists of three sold comparables and three active/list comparables. Under contract properties may be used as list comparables. From the comparables generated from the MLS, choose the 3 best sold comps and the 3 best list comps.

b) Make every attempt to locate sold/list comparables that are equal to the subject in style, size, features, location, etc. It is preferable to stay within the same subdivision or multifamily complex when possible. It is also preferable to compare ranches to ranches, 2 stories to 2 stories, etc.

c) Make every effort to bracket the subject by finding a superior, approximately equal and an inferior property for your comparables.

d) Bracket each sold/list comp as superior, equal, and inferior.

Income=BPO Simplified, Presented by James A. Browning

e) Determine distance for each comp from subject in miles or blocks.

Four Parameters

a) Comps to be within 1 mile or explanation required.

b) Comps to be + or – 25% of the square footage of the subject.

c) Comps to be + or – 15 years of subject's age (YOC).

d) Comps to be 6 months old or less, or explanation required.

Adjustments

Adjustments are required when the comparable and subject property differ. Adjustments are made to the comparable and never to the subject. You are attempting to adjust the comparable to make it similar to the subject. When a comparable is inferior to the subject, you add value to the comparable, and when a comparable is superior to the subject, you subtract value from the comparable.

Adjustments are most commonly made when there is a difference between subject and comparable in:

- square footage (above ground only)

- number of bedrooms (above ground only)

- number of bathrooms (above ground only)

- general condition

- style of home

- basement (none, unfinished, finished, etc.)

- quality of construction

- concessions (these will always be entered as a negative adjustment)

- year of construction (YOC)/age

- lot size

- location and views (urban, suburban, rural, mountain view, corner lot, open space views, etc.)

- features and physical characteristics (patio, porch, fireplace, air conditioning, upgrades, etc)

(Client specifications always take precedence over information provided.)

As we complete the adjustment worksheet, you will see how and why these adjustments are made. Adjustment amounts do not match the actual replacement cost. For example, if the average price per square foot in a neighborhood is $100.00, you do not use $100.00. It would be more likely you would use somewhere in the range of $20.00 to $40.00 per square foot.

Feature	Subject	+/-	Comparable	=	Diff. X Feature	= $ Adjustment
Garage	1		2		1 x $3,000	- $3,000

Entering Information on the BPO form

It is advisable to have all required information prior to working on the BPO. You will want to have your subject property information, comps selected with distances from subject, original list price, original list date, days on market, lot size, etc. ready. You do not want to stop and look up information for each comp once you begin data entry. Should you have numerous BPO assignments due, you must work smart in order to meet your deadlines.

- Enter all requested information about the subject property.

- In most cases you are asked to describe the property – describe in detail. If the BPO does not specifically ask for this information, find someplace to describe the property.

- There is usually a section for neighborhood information as well as a description of the market area. You must be objective in all comments. Never use subjective statements. Your comments must be verifiable and cannot violate any fair housing practices.

- Basements & Crawlspaces: If the property has any area below natural grade, this is considered below grade and not included in the finished square footage. This area should be noted and valued separately. It is recommended to take photos of this area, and record any comments.

- Enter comparables from the best to the least. The best comparable is in the first place, the next best in the second place, and the third position is for the least similar comparable.

- List prices are not the best indicator of value as there is often little consistency in pricing. For example, prices can be under market value if the listing is a short sale, and may not even reflect what a lender will accept. Prices can be over inflated in cases where sellers are not motivated to sell, or have unrealistic expectations of what their properties are worth. The only time list prices may reflect the current state of the market is when list prices are noticeably and consistently lower than solds in the last 6 months, or under contract and significantly higher than solds in the last 6 months.

- BPO Comments: For each comparable, you will be required to enter comments. Remember you are the eyes and ears for the client. Comments on condition, adjustments made, and terms of sale/financing are guidelines to follow. You do not need to state information already provided elsewhere. It is advisable to comment on additional bedrooms/baths in basement and other features not listed elsewhere on the BPO.

- Many forms will ask you to rate the comparables, as inferior, equal or superior. Often they will ask you to identify the list and sold comparable most similar to the subject.

- Repaired price for the subject: If the subject is in poor or fair condition, then comps that are in good condition can be used to determine a repaired price for the subject.

Land Value

Many BPOs ask for the value of the land on which an asset sits. Typically you will want to find comps with similar size lots or acreage. There will also be opportunities to do BPOs on vacant land, subdivision lots, etc. The sales comparable method and allocation method will be discussed:

Sales Comparable Approach:
Sales of similar size lots or land parcels are analyzed and compared. When valuing land, the sales comp approach provides the best method to analyze the market value of the land. It may be very difficult to find sale comparables that are in the same vicinity or in a small radius of the subject; no two lots are identical in size or shape. Your job is to find the most probable value of the subject property by interpreting records and data from the recent sales of similar properties. For vacant land BPOS, find recent sales comps on vacant properties, because no two parcels of land are normally identical.

The real estate broker will have to adjust for some differences when comparing sold properties to the subject property.

Typical differences include:

- Financing/Conditions of Sale

- Date of Sale (should be within 6 months & within 3 months, rapid market)

- Location (Subdivision/Sub Area, Neighborhood)

- Correct Zoning and Zoning Restrictions, Permitted Land Use

- Land Characteristics (square feet, shape, topography)

Allocation Approach:
To determine the land value for residential properties, the allocation approach is a common method.

Land value may be treated as a percentage of the total value for an improved asset. Most residential areas have a 1 to 4 land to building value ratio or can be expressed in a percentage of 25%. The land value is 25% of the total value of the property. For example: The total value of the property (house and land) is $100,000, 25% of $100,000 =$25,000. The land value is $25,000.
As demand for buildable land increases and the supply of land decreases, the ratio of land to building value tends to narrow as their values come closer together. The 1 to 4 ratio may

become 1 to 3 (33%) or even 1 to 2 (50%). This occurs because the cost of land rises and the cost of developing the land rises. (roads, infrastructure, curbs, gutters, sidewalks, utilities etc…)

Repairs

Most BPOs will ask you to itemize repairs needed and the cost. When doing an exterior BPO, you can only comment on exterior repairs. It is usually safe to assume that the interior condition will be similar to the exterior condition; however since you have not viewed the interior you cannot make repair comments. When doing an interior BPO, you must comment on both exterior and interior repairs. There will be times when you are asked to initially complete an exterior BPO for a subject property and then, at a later date, complete an interior BPO. Lenders understand that if the condition of the interior is significantly different than the exterior that your values may change. Should this be the case, as always, provide a descriptive explanation as to why your values have changed.

Itemize ALL repairs needed to bring the property from its present "AS IS" condition to average marketable/lendable condition for the neighborhood. Typically repairs should be targeted to an FHA buyer, however you will encounter properties where the most likely buyer will be an investor and repairs are then not recommended. Check those repairs you recommend be performed for the most successful marketing of the property. Do not make the mistake of providing repairs over and above average marketable/lendable condition. For example, if carpet cleaning would work, recommend this as opposed to carpet replacement. If carpet needs to be replaced, you will want to estimate the replacement cost for FHA grade carpet, not anything superior. If you notice a hazardous condition or code violation at the property, you will want to make note of this and also email your contact about this. Some BPO forms will also ask you to check recommended inspections, such as roof, plumbing, electrical, systems, etc.

Most BPO forms will ask if there is evidence of mold or water damage. You will want to pay particular attention to this upon interior inspection.

Should your BPO turn into a listing, you may be asked to provide bids for repairs, so it is advisable to begin to compile a list of vendors list that you can contact for pricing and repair work.

Almost all properties will need at a minimum, a sales clean, initial landscape and yard clean up and biweekly grass cut. Examples of these costs are as follows:

Item	Estimated Cost
Sales Clean	$250.00
Yard Clean	$175.00
Grass Cut	$75.00

GRAND TOTAL FOR REPAIRS: $500.00

NOTE: We do not offer repair recommendations in this book, repairs vary by location and contractors prices for completion of work.

Marketing Strategy

The outsourcer might request a marketing strategy for the subject property. There will be a section on the BPO to select a strategy and comment on the strategy as well. You will want to include what you would do to sell this property within a 30 – 90 day timeframe, aside from placing property in the MLS and planting a sign.

There may also be a place for you to check in what condition the property should be sold: as is, minimal lender repairs or repaired. They may also ask you who the most likely buyer will be: owner occupant, first time homebuyer, move –up buyer or investor.

Pricing

The last step in the BPO process is to reconcile your information and assign a value to the subject property.

Final prices are to be rounded to the nearest $1,000 while adjustments are to be rounded to the nearest $100.

- It is at this point where you check relevancy and accuracy of the data compiled, and then arrive at a price.

- This is where your professional opinion and judgment is called upon to price the property based on all the facts that have been gathered.

- Reconciliation is the final statement of reasoning and weighting of relative importance of all facts, the results and your conclusion to arrive at a price.

- Check and consider the following when reconciling:

  a) Calculations, the accuracy

  b) Consistent use of criteria for all comps

  c) Adjustments, consistent values

  d) Data collected, reliability and accuracy

  e) Comp to the Subject, similarities/differences

  f) Your final opinion of value must fall between your lowest and highest adjusted sales comps values.

Using your comparable adjustments

The prices for each comp should be similar after ADJUSTMENTS are provided.

The real estate professional will have to formulate the price for each comp in order to arrive at the price for the subject. There is no exact science for reconciling the indicated price of the comparables. Judgment and careful analysis by the broker is imperative.

Alternative Pricing Methods

There are several other methods that the broker may use. Average adjusted values should only be used when comps are very similar to the subject:

Adjusted Sale Price

Comp # 1	$138.000
Comp # 2	$143,000
Comp # 3	$146,000
Average	$142,333

Average price per square foot

Another common method is the average adjusted price per square foot. Determine the average price per square foot for each comp and apply that average to the subject's square footage. MLS summary statistics for the subject's market area will also provide you with an average price per square foot as well.

	SF	Adjusted Sales Price	PSF
Comp # 1	1800	$275,000	$152.77
Comp # 2	1900	$295,000	$155.26
Comp # 3	1950	$310,000	$158.97

Square Foot Average $155.66

Subject   1888 X $155.66 = $293,886.08 = Subject's Value

Reconcile

Please feel free to use one or all of these methods to arrive at a final value for the BPO. Before submitting the final values, consider the following:

- supply and demand trends

- subdivision, neighborhood, state, regional and local economic factors

- market conditions

- unemployment

- the current lending environment

- Do NOT overvalue the subject thinking you will get a listing if you value the property high. Your accuracy in the actual suggested sales price to the final eventual sales price is typically the most important factor in receiving a continual stream of REO properties.

Common Value Categories

You will be asked to provide several different values on your BPO.
They are commonly referred to as, "As Is", "Repaired Value" and "Quick Sale Value". Your final values must fall between your lowest and highest adjusted sales comps.

"As is" and "repaired" pricing will be the same, if no repairs are recommended. This is often the case with an exterior BPO.

"As Is"

This is the price that you give to the property without making any changes or repairs to the property. Essentially, this is the price that you arrive at without any consideration. If there is apparent damage to the property or repairs needed, it is very important to price the property at a price a potential buyer would pay for the property, "as is"; not by deducting the repair cost from the base price.

"Repaired"

If a property does not have any apparent damage or is not in need of repair, this value will be the same as "as is". If a property has apparent damage, this is what the price would be as if the property was repaired. The BPO form calls for costs to repair the property – this is a separate consideration and should not be confused with the price of the subject. Remember that the cost of repairs may not increase the value by the same amount as the cost; the price may be more or it may be less.

"Quick Sale"

This is the price that you need in order to sell the property "as is" quickly. The price will be noticeably **Lower than Market Price**. Supply and demand is an important factor in determining the price. In a balanced market, a property with a normal asking price of $225K may need to be listed at $215K in order for a quick sale. In a market with a high demand, the same property would get a quick sale if it was listed at $220K, whereas in a market with a high supply, the property may need to be listed at $190K to get a quick sale.

Comments

You will have several sections on the BPO where you can comment on the property. The more information provided the better. If necessary you can attach an additional page of notes when you upload your BPO. The key is to be very descriptive about the property, the area, and the market. Detail how far the subject property is from the major downtown area, highway, schools, parks, retail, industrial, and airport. Comment on any data that describes the subdivision or area. These should be objective facts with no subjective terms. Comments are to always be concise and objective including market conditions, employment, and trends. MLS comments are normally subjective. Comment on anything that needs further clarification or justification. For example, if there are no closed sales in the subject's neighborhood and you had to go outside of the area, or outside a one mile radius, comment as to why you did this. When in doubt, explain and expand.

Photos

As the client's "eyes", accurate photos must be taken. Only the data entered into the BPO form, and the supporting photos will provide an accurate story for the outsourcer. Our recommendation is to take 40-60 pictures for an interior BPO and 5-10 for an exterior BPO. You can never take too many photos to tell the biography of the asset. The more data you have, the more you limit your liability. Make sure that your photos are clear, do not include people or pets in the photos, and follow assignment instructions if your photos are to have a date and time stamp. Resizing of photographs will be required. Most systems have maximum size requirements.

* These are guidelines for both Exterior and Interior BPOs.

Exterior Photos

a) Front View- Take at least two front exterior photos. You can take a full front on view, and also one from a 45 degree angle. This will allow you to photograph the asset's corners, and placement on the lot.
b) Street Scene- Take a photo from each direction, while standing in front/curb of the property. If located on a cul-de-sac, corner, or the street has a feature that you need to record make sure to include that as well.
c) Street Sign- As an accurate record, you should photograph the city posted street sign. The name should be readable. This will help should you be photographing numerous properties prior to downloading them to your computer.
d) Address Verification- Zoom in to photograph the house number on the property. If you are unable to get a clear picture, record the number on the mailbox, or painted on the curb.
e) Additional Exterior Photos- Side views, fence, backyard or rear exterior if visible, as well as any visible features that would detail the asset. Make sure to include any visible damage if any.

Interior Photos

a) All Rooms- Photographs should be taken of all rooms in the home. In order to make an accurate record, more than one photograph of a room may be necessary. (Example: Large family room with fireplace or built-ins. Take a photo of the room, and an additional photo showing the feature.)
b) Additional Interior Photos- Take photographs of anything that will affect the value of the home. This would include upgrades, remodeling, damage and deferred maintenance. Also record if any items are missing from the property. (Example: stove, compressor, cabinets, etc.)
c) Systems- It is recommended to take photographs of all systems in the asset. This includes heating/cooling, sprinkler system, hot water heater, electric box, sump pump, and water softener.

d) Labeling Photos- Make sure that the photo shows an accurate depiction of the label assigned to it.

Make sure that all photographs are current. If you are requested to revisit the home for any reason, make sure to take a new set of photos. If the condition of the home changes at any time, you will want to record this to inform the client. Damage can occur to an asset that may need immediate attention. You represent the client, and the asset is your potential income.

BPO Submission & Record Keeping

Accepting a BPO

When accepting a BPO, adhering to timelines for completion are mandatory. If the outsourcer demands a completion period of 72 hours, complete the BPO early. DO NOT request an extension unless you have a situation that is a hardship. If you cannot complete all tasks on-line, on-time, it is better not to accept the BPO. Outsourcers will understand that scenario better than an incomplete and/or late BPO. First impressions or the first BPO, are extremely important. This may be the only time that you receive the opportunity to perform a BPO. DO NOT make a mistake; it may be your only opportunity. Your performance will be graded based on turnaround time, overall performance, and accuracy. If orders are consistently late, your BPO income will disappear. Communicate with your outsourcer, but do so via email. This will generate the quickest response. Be aware that your outsourcer may be in a different time zone. Be mindful of this, and make sure that all communication and tasks are completed by the end of the business day in their time zone.

Your BPO records should be kept for a minimum of one year from completion.

How do you increase your income by completing BPOs?

BPO Application Process

In the reference section of this manual, you will find a list of companies looking for Brokers to complete BPOs.

For most companies to become an approved BPO agent, you will need to provide the following
- 2 years of experience
- 3 references
- Real Estate or Appraiser license
- W9
- E&O Insurance with an aggregate amount of $300,000 to $1,000,000 depending on client

You will need to provide copies of
- State License
- Resume
- E&O Policy
- Signed and dated W9

The criteria required may vary from company to company. The requirements for becoming a REO Broker will be discussed later in the book.

Potential Income and Fee information

During this time and market of distressed properties, real estate professionals are looking for ways to supplement their income. With the staggering rate of foreclosures, the banks/lenders/outsourcers are literally over-run with property portfolios on a daily basis. These properties need to be re-valued daily on the open market.

There is not a maximum amount of income you can earn completing BPOs. This will entirely depend on how often the real estate professional will work or how the broker sets up the office system to meet the demand for BPOs.

For example: There are Broker BPO factories that complete 2,000 to 6,000 BPOs per year. These companies can generate thousands of dollars of income per year. Let's stay on the lower end of 2,000 BPOs annually x $55.00 (average) = $110,000 of income.

Each lender/outsourcer will offer their BPOs for completion via the computer. The broker will have to accept or reject their offer to complete the BPO by a certain time and date. Many opportunities will be generated by outsourcers and the broker has to accept or reject offers sometimes within seconds or minutes.

BPO fees range by what the lenders/outsourcers offer. Exterior BPO fees can be anywhere from $45.00 to $100.00 depending on the location, type and what the outsourcer demands as to how detailed the BPO should be. Interior BPO fees can range from $55.00 to $150.00 and again the fees are according to what the lenders/outsourcers demand.

Some outsourcers will ask the real estate professional to perform a BPO for free, and then they promise to assign you this property should it turn into a listing. Be careful, as some companies will promise you the moon. It is entirely your decision which lenders/outsourcers with whom you choose to partner.

- Complete comparables and adjustment worksheet in the book.

Feature	Subject	+/-	Comparable	=	Diff. X Feature	= $ Adjustment
Bedroom	2		3		1 x $2,000	- $2,000

Remember to adjust your comparable to match your subject. The scenario above shows the comp having one more bedroom than subject, so comp is adjusted -$2,000.

Scenario for Adjustment Worksheet and Comparables

These are guidelines used for this book. Adjust according to your market and condition.

Feature	$ Adjustment
Age/YOC	$500 per year
Bedroom	$2,000
Bath	$1,500
Heating/Cooling	$1,500 AC, $1,000 Evap Cooler
Garage	$3,000
Fireplace	$1,000

Subject: 1423 Quivas Dr.

Address	1423 Quivas Dr
Location	Suburban
Lot Size	4,000 SF
View	Street, None
Design	Ranch
Square Feet	1,000
Age	45
Condition	Good
Bedrooms	3
Baths	2
Basement	None
Heating/Cooling	GFA, AC
Garage/Carport	1 Car Attached Garage
Porch,Patio,Fireplace,etc.	Fireplace
Fence,Pool,etc.	Fence

Use this data to complete the adjustment worksheet, on the following comparables.

Sold Comp #1 – 1260 Simpson Ave

Address	1260 Simpson Ave
Proximity to Subject	.08 miles
Sold Price	$175,000
Concessions	$3,000 Slr Pd Closing Costs
Sold Date/Days On Market	Sold 8 days ago, 178 DOM
Location	Suburban
Lot Size	4,000 SF
View	Street, None
Design	Ranch
Square Feet	980
Age	47
Condition	Good
Bedrooms	3
Baths	2
Basement	None
Heating/Cooling	GFA, None
Garage/Carport	1 Car Attached Garage
Porch,Patio,Fireplace,etc.	2 Fireplaces
Fence,Pool,etc.	Fence

Adjustment Worksheet

Feature	Subj	-	Comp	=	Difference	x	Feature Value	=	$ Adjustment
Age	45	-		=		x		=	$
Bdrm	3	-		=		x		=	$
Bath	2	-		=		x		=	$
HVAC	AC	-		=		x		=	$
Garage	1	-		=		x		=	$
Fireplace	1	-		=		x		=	$

Total Adjustment $_____

Sold Price - Concessions +/- Adjustment = $_____
_____ - _____ +/- _____ = $_____
Inferior ☐ Superior ☐ Equal ☐

Income=BPO Simplified, Presented by James A. Browning

Sold Comp #2 – 1399 Lemont Ave

Address	1399 Lemont Ave
Proximity to Subject	.28 miles
Sold Price	$163,000
Concessions	$0
Sold Date/Days On Market	Sold 183 days ago, 240 DOM
Location	Suburban
Lot Size	3,200 SF
View	Mountains
Design	Ranch
Square Feet	1,020
Age	55
Condition	Good
Bedrooms	3
Baths	2
Basement	None
Heating/Cooling	GFA, Evap Cooler
Garage/Carport	2 Car Attached Garage
Porch,Patio,Fireplace,etc.	1 Fireplace
Fence,Pool,etc.	Fence

Adjustment Worksheet

Feature	Subj	-	Comp	=	Difference	x	Feature Value	=	$ Adjustment
Age	45	-		=		x		=	$
Bdrm	3	-		=		x		=	$
Bath	2	-		=		x		=	$
HVAC	AC	-		=		x		=	$
Garage	1	-		=		x		=	$
Fireplace	1	-		=		x		=	$

Total Adjustment $_____

Sold Price - Concessions +/- Adjustment = $_____
_____ - _____ +/- _____ = $_____

Inferior □ Superior □ Equal □

Sold Comp #3 – 1345 Black Hawk St.

Address	1345 Black Hawk St
Proximity to Subject	1.23 miles
Sold Price	$167,000
Concessions	$2,100 Slr Pd Closing Costs
Sold Date/Days On Market	Sold 89 days ago, 120 DOM
Location	Suburban
Lot Size	3,115 SF
View	Street, None
Design	Ranch
Square Feet	1,035
Age	37
Condition	Good
Bedrooms	4
Baths	3
Basement	None
Heating/Cooling	GFA, None
Garage/Carport	1 Car Attached Garage
Porch,Patio,Fireplace,etc.	1 Fireplace
Fence,Pool,etc.	Fence

Adjustment Worksheet

Feature	Subj	-	Comp	=	Difference	x	Feature Value	=	$ Adjustment
Age	45	-		=		x		=	$
Bdrm	3	-		=		x		=	$
Bath	2	-		=		x		=	$
HVAC	AC	-		=		x		=	$
Garage	1	-		=		x		=	$
Fireplace	1	-		=		x		=	$

Total Adjustment $_____

Sold Price - Concessions +/- Adjustment = $_____
_____ - _____ +/- _____ = $_____
Inferior ☐ Superior ☐ Equal ☐

Income=BPO Simplified, Presented by James A. Browning

List Comp #1 – 1299 Forest Way

Address	1299 Forest Way
Proximity to Subject	1.2 miles
List Price	$179,900
Concessions	None
Days On Market	15 DOM
Location	Suburban
Lot Size	3,144 SF
View	Street, None
Design	Two Story
Square Feet	1,050
Age	40
Condition	Good
Bedrooms	3
Baths	2
Basement	None
Heating/Cooling	GFA, Evap Cooler
Garage/Carport	2 Car Attached Garage
Porch,Patio,Fireplace,etc.	1 Fireplace
Fence,Pool,etc.	Fence

Adjustment Worksheet

Feature	Subj	-	Comp	=	Difference	x	Feature Value	=	$ Adjustment
Age	45	-		=		x		=	$
Bdrm	3	-		=		x		=	$
Bath	2	-		=		x		=	$
HVAC	AC	-		=		x		=	$
Garage	1	-		=		x		=	$
Fireplace	1	-		=		x		=	$

Total Adjustment $_____

List Price - Concessions +/- Adjustment = $_____
_____ - _____ +/- _____ = $_____

Inferior ☐ Superior ☐ Equal ☐

List Comp #2 – 1278 Walters Ave

Address	1278 Walters Ave
Proximity to Subject	.67 miles
List Price	$163,000
Concessions	None
Days On Market	185 DOM
Location	Suburban
Lot Size	3,200 SF
View	Street, None
Design	Ranch
Square Feet	1,095
Age	45
Condition	Good
Bedrooms	4
Baths	2
Basement	None
Heating/Cooling	GFA, None
Garage/Carport	None
Porch,Patio,Fireplace,etc.	None
Fence,Pool,etc.	Fence

Adjustment Worksheet

Feature	Subj	-	Comp	=	Difference	x	Feature Value	=	$ Adjustment
Age	45	-		=		x		=	$
Bdrm	3	-		=		x		=	$
Bath	2	-		=		x		=	$
HVAC	AC	-		=		x		=	$
Garage	1	-		=		x		=	$
Fireplace	1	-		=		x		=	$

Total Adjustment $_____

List Price - Concessions +/- Adjustment = $_____

_____ - _____ +/- _____ = $_____

Inferior ☐   Superior ☐   Equal ☐

Income=BPO Simplified, Presented by James A. Browning

List Comp #3 – 2381 74ᵗʰ Pl.

Address	2381 74ᵗʰ Pl.
Proximity to Subject	.09 miles
List Price	$137,900
Concessions	None
Days On Market	56 DOM
Location	Suburban
Lot Size	2,890 SF
View	Street, None
Design	Ranch
Square Feet	975
Age	58
Condition	Fair
Bedrooms	2
Baths	2
Basement	None
Heating/Cooling	GFA, AC
Garage	1 Car Attached Garage
Porch,Patio,Fireplace,etc.	None
Fence,Pool,etc.	Fence

Adjustment Worksheet

Feature	Subj	-	Comp	=	Difference	x	Feature Value	=	$ Adjustment
Age	45	-		=		x		=	$
Bdrm	3	-		=		x		=	$
Bath	2	-		=		x		=	$
HVAC	AC	-		=		x		=	$
Garage	1	-		=		x		=	$
Fireplace	1	-		=		x		=	$

Total Adjustment $_____

List Price - Concessions +/- Adjustment = $_____

_____ - _____ +/- _____ = $_____

Inferior ☐ Superior ☐ Equal ☐

INCOME = REO SIMPLIFIED

What is a REO Property?

REO is "Real Estate Owned". These are properties that have gone through the foreclosure process without any type of successful sale (for example, short sale) and revert back to the lender, mortgage company or bank. These properties can be:

    a. Single Family dwellings
    b. Land or lots
    c. Duplexes
    d. Townhouses
    e. Condos

Banks do not want to own these properties. They stand to lose more money on property ownership than on lending money. Therefore, they want to dispose of these properties by hiring people who have the right skill set and experience.

Who can perform REOs?

Realtors, brokers, agents, and active licensees can list REOs. If you are considering performing REOs, this must be discussed with your employing broker and/or attorney to determine the ramifications of performing REOs in your specific state or market area.

Criteria for becoming a REO Broker:

- Have an active license within your state
- Carry the appropriate amount of E & O Insurance as required by your clients
- 3 – 5 years of REO experience
- Education in the field of REO, professional designations
- Zip code coverage area which you can effectively work and service
- 3 – 5 client referrals/references
- Network of professional/honest vendors
- Excellent sales and marketing skills as well as professionalism
- Cash reserves to cover the cost of carrying and maintaining multiple properties. Your clients will require you to pay for services up front, and then you will be reimbursed. This could take anywhere from 30 – 90 days.
- Tool kit including bolt cutter. Don't be afraid to fix minor things or get your hands dirty
- Appropriate technology and equipment, including multi-page scanner

What is an Outsourcer?

This is either a division of a financial institution or a stand alone company. They are also considered to be the client. Whereas some banks have their own internal departments that manage their properties, others choose to outsource this function to asset management firms who handle these properties from assignment through sale.

The first step is to sign up with banks, outsourcers, and asset management companies. Company specific applications will ask for:

- REO experience
- Completed IRS W-9 form
- Resume
- Copy of real estate license and E & O Insurance
- Zip code coverage area list
- References

Once approved, you will be required to sign a Master Listing Agreement.

- This Agreement outlines the basic operating procedures and expectations for each client. Quite often, if you encounter a situation where you are unsure what to do, you can refer back to the Master Listing Agreement for your clients' guidelines.

Expectations of the Outsourcer/Asset Management Company/Bank

- Understand how to work with Asset Managers, your responsibilities and your accountability.
- Completion of all tasks on time.
- Ability to read and follow directions. They do not want to hold your hand.
- Accuracy in pricing properties.
- Completion of monthly marketing reports and updated BPOs on a timely basis.
- Professional and honest network of contractors/subcontractors for the preservation of properties. Many clients will require up to three different bids, depending on total cost for repair, replacement, trash out and any work that needs to be performed.
- Submission of invoices for reimbursement in a timely manner.
- The client is always right.
- Market knowledge.
- Ability to market property, following the guidelines that are required. REO properties need unique marketing efforts. Knowledge of the auction process and where and how to list properties on various websites is needed.
- Initial and ongoing property maintenance and management.
- Sufficient capital funds to cover utilities, HOA payments, past due taxes if required, repairs, evictions, bringing property to marketable condition and ongoing maintenance.
- Willingness to work whatever hours necessary to get the job done.
- Creativeness in marketing properties and getting properties sold with minimal contract cancellations.
- A "no excuse" mentality. Just get the job done. Don't complain.

The challenges of becoming a REO broker

Do the positives outweigh the negatives? Listed below are things to consider prior to committing to this line of work.

Negatives
- More work required for each property. There is ongoing maintenance and monitoring. You need to understand what repairs need to be done and oversee this process. You will need to connect, maintain and pay for all utilities.
- More responsibility. As the sole point of contact, you are responsible for any issues that arise such as vandalism, broken pipes, missing lockbox keys, code violations, neighborhood complaints, etc.
- More paperwork. There are bank addenda, updated BPOs, monthly reports, delayed reimbursements.
- Lower commissions. This is not negotiable. Outsourcers collect referral fees. If you don't like the commission, don't take the assignment or choose not to work with that particular company.

Positives
- If you are good, be prepared for a steady stream of listings. Word of mouth referral is the best way to increase your business. Do a good job for one Asset Manager, and they will pass your name on. Asset Managers change companies and love to bring their experienced agents to their new companies as well.
- Non-emotional sale. There is no homeowner to deal with. You are given directions, and you follow them.
- Once you learn the routine of what is expected, you develop systems which are easy to follow.
- Lower commissions but more closings.

How to work with Asset Managers?

- Asset Managers expect you to be an expert in your area and to know what needs to be done to sell properties.
- Be professional and prepared. Understand their work load. Whereas you may have 10 listings, keep in mind the average Asset Manager portfolio ranges from 200 – 400 properties. Always consider solutions for problems in advance of contacting them. Take the initiative to resolve things not needing their attention. For example, should you arrive at one of your properties and find two tires dumped on the front yard, just remove them yourself, instead of contacting the Asset Manager for approval to get bids for removal. Never complain. They don't want to hear about it and you will be remembered for being whiny. Always communicate via email whenever possible. Be respectful of their time. Be patient while waiting for their response. Do not keep reminding them you are awaiting their response.

THE REO ASSET MANAGEMENT PROCESS

Each of your clients may have slightly different guidelines, timelines and criteria; however there is a typical and logical flow to the REO property process. Once a property is assigned to a REO broker, the property becomes that broker's responsibility from "cradle to grave" or from assignment through close.

Initial assignment through securing of property

a. **Assignment of the REO listing.** REOs are most often assigned based on your experience, registration with that particular outsourcer and on your zip code service area. The assignment letter will detail expectations, timelines, and tasks. Read these letters very carefully as they will usually provide all needed information. You may be asked to accept the assignment in writing. There are often initial forms which are attached to the initial assignment letter. These could be for occupant information, personal property information or initial/exterior condition inspection. Typical timeframe to accept is 24 hours.

b. **Complete an occupancy check.** Initially, the client wants to know if the property is occupied or vacant. Occupancy checks may be requested on properties still going through the foreclosure process or properties which have been fully foreclosed upon. If a property is vacant and still going through the foreclosure process, in most states, the bank has the right to preserve the asset which means they could request a front or rear door rekey only and winterization if appropriate. Typical timeframe to perform an occupancy check is 24 hours. Weekends are not excluded.

c. **If vacant**, the outsourcer will request information on personal property remaining. You may be requested to itemize contents and place a garage sale value on contents. Different states have different requirements on what constitutes a personal property eviction, however over $300.00 in garage sale value is typically used for this type of eviction. If vacant and appropriate to do so, rekey and secure property. Typical timeframe is 24 – 48 hours to complete this task.

d. **If property is occupied and still in the foreclosure process**, you may be asked to inspect the property on a weekly or bi-weekly basis and report on any changes of status. At this point you may be asked to perform an exterior BPO.

e. **If occupied, and the property is foreclosed upon**, the outsourcer will ask the broker to contact the occupants to determine if they are the prior owners of record or tenants. You should never attempt to contact the occupant unless specifically instructed to do so by your client.

f. **Cash for keys** may be offered to occupants. The amount and timeframe varies by client. As the broker, you are expected to successfully negotiate as many cash for keys as possible. Properties must be left free and clear of all personal property, trash, lawn maintained and left in broom swept clean condition. Don't forget to check attics, crawl spaces, sheds, etc. The bank will ask the broker to negotiate with all occupants of the property over the age of 18. They will advise you how much to offer to assist the occupants with relocation. It is not uncommon for a 2 week period to be offered. Occupants are not allowed to remove attached items, such as appliances, unless they can provide a receipt showing their proof of purchase. In addition, the interior and exterior condition of the property cannot change from the date the cash for keys agreement was negotiated. On the negotiated date and time, you will meet the occupants at the property along with a locksmith to exchange the check for keys, rekey and secure the property. Should you provide the cash for keys check to the occupants, and they have not met all of the required conditions, you as the broker will be required to pay for any remaining trash out, etc. Should you arrive at the property on the predetermined move out date to turn over the check, and all conditions have not been met, the agreement is immediately terminated.

g. **Tenant Occupied:** There are very specific tenant rights which the REO broker must know. If a property is occupied by tenants, tenants may have the right to remain in the property until the conclusion of their lease. However there are specific guidelines which must be followed. Tenants must be able to produce 6 months of rent receipts, have a bona fide lease (arms length transaction) which was signed prior to the notice of election and demand being filed. The goal of the outsourcer, bank, or lender is to take possession of the property as quickly as possible. Therefore they may choose to offer a more significant cash for keys incentive to tenants.

h. **Ongoing inspections of foreclosed occupied properties:** If a property is occupied, you should be prepared to inspect the property on an ongoing basis. Typically your client will ask you to inspect the property bi-weekly and to notify them of any changes to occupancy.

i. **Eviction:** No matter what, the cash for keys agreement must be negotiated with a move out date prior to an official eviction ordered through the courts. Even if the cash for keys is negotiated, the eviction will still continue through the courts. In the event the cash for keys is not successful, the eviction does not then need to be restarted. Should the property have an actual eviction, it is your responsibility to meet the sheriff at the property at the assigned time. You will need a moving crew large enough to move all contents out of the property in a one hour time period. Size of crew will depend on size of home, number of rooms, and amount of personal property. In addition, you will need to have a locksmith at the property at the same time to change the locks and secure the property. Each client will have different requirements as to who handles some of these tasks. It could be the REO broker or it could be a national preservation company.

j. **Exterior and Interior inspection and BPO preparation:** Once you have taken possession of the property, you will complete a full inspection, making a thorough set of notes on every detail about the property. For example:

- All mechanical systems
- HVAC systems
- Furnace
- Hot water heater
- Water purifier
- Sprinkler system
- Electrical panel
- Condition and working order of appliances
- Missing lights, vanities, toilets, ceiling fans, faucets, etc
- Damage, holes in walls, missing doors
- Water leaks and damage

- Mold or standing water
- Condition of roof and/or damage
- Condition of the siding/brick exterior
- Any cracks in walls, ceilings or floors
- Foundation issues
- Exterior issues, cracked driveway, sidewalk
- Broken or cracked windows
- Specific type of flooring, carpet, paint, fireplaces, patios, decks, upgrades, etc
- Specifics of each room
- Research and verify flood zone status, taxes due, liens, outstanding HOA/utility bills, unresolved permits and city, county or state ordinance violations

k. **Photos:** As the "eyes and ears" for the bank/outsourcers, accurate photos are required. We recommend that the broker take between 40 – 60 photos of the subject property on the first inspection and every time you revisit the property. By documenting everything in writing and by camera, you will be prepared to do your interior BPO.

*Specific guidelines and sample photos are discussed in the BPO Simplified section.

- **<u>Interior Photos- make sure all are labeled</u>**
- Take 2 photos of each room
- Take at least 3 – 4 photos of the kitchen
- All rooms
- All systems

- **<u>Exterior Photos- make sure all are labeled</u>**
- Front view
- Street scene
- Street sign
- Address verification
- All sides of the house
- Backyard

Property preservation and maintenance

As was stated previously, your assigned properties belong to you from "cradle to grave", or from assignment to closing. You may be required to manage property preservation and maintenance, or your client may outsource this to a national preservation vendor. It is very important that you understand your clients' expectations. If you are asked to manage this process, you will be given guidelines as to maximum cost for each service (rekey, winterization, lawn cuts, trash out, etc). In addition, you will be told when bids are required and how many, based on the cost for each service. The experienced REO broker will anticipate these tasks and be proactive in starting these steps early.

a. **Securing the property:** Always refer to your clients' guidelines as to required key code and lockbox requirements. Pay careful attention to the amount you can spend on a rekey and what your client wants rekeyed. Some want every exterior lock rekeyed, as well as the door from the house to garage. Other clients may not want anything but the front door rekeyed. Make sure all windows are locked, sliding doors are secured, and any broken windows are immediately boarded up. Make sure the garage door and all entrances to the basement are secured. It is always a good idea to have an extra set of keys. They have a way of disappearing!

b. **Winterizations:** All clients will have specific requirements for winterizations and dates when winterizations must be done. Typically it is from September 30 – April 30 in freeze zones. You will need to learn the difference between wet and dry winterizations. At the very least, when taking possession of a property, make sure the water main is turned off. If possible, make sure the heat is running until a property can be winterized. You will want to hire a plumbing or HVAC specialist who understands what needs to be done to successfully winterize a property. They will need to be bonded and licensed. The cost for this procedure varies by region. You will need to submit a completed winterization document. By signing this document you state the winterization is complete, and your clients' guidelines have been followed. Improper winterizations could mean you are liable for the repairs.

c. **Obtain trash out, initial lawn clean up, interior cleaning bids:** You will be required to submit bids for full interior and exterior trash out, initial yard and lawn clean up, and interior cleaning. Depending on the cost, you may be required to submit 1 – 3 bids. Be proactive and get these bids as soon as possible. Do not wait until tasked to do so, as you are quite often only given 48 – 72 hours to get the bids. Contractors will need to be bonded and insured. You should also request bids for any other obvious repairs that are needed at the same time.

d. **Lawn maintenance:** Most clients will ask for biweekly lawn maintenance and provide specific guidelines as to the amount that can be spent. Some clients will ask that sprinkler systems run in HOA communities to avoid fines. Refer to your specific assignment letter.

e. **Snow removal:** Snow removal is done on an as needed basis. Again, you are usually told what the maximum cost can be. Remember, you are responsible for ensuring safe conditions at each property. You do not want your client or yourself to be held liable for someone falling at a property due to lack of snow removal. In addition, you do not want your property to be cited for a code violation.

f. **Preserving the asset:** You must make sure that each property is secured and in safe condition. This means if a window is broken, you need to get it boarded up. If there is a water leak, you must take charge immediately to preserve the asset. Your clients will let you know what their procedures are. Quite often, you are expected to do whatever is necessary to preserve the asset, and notify your client immediately. If it is after hours, you will be expected to call an emergency number, or leave a message for your asset manager and also email at the same time. Photo document everything. Specific guidelines can usually be found in the Master Listing Agreement or Assignment Letter.

g. **Repairs:** You are required to document and itemize all repairs needed to bring the property to FHA lendable condition. This does not necessarily mean the client will choose to do these repairs, but you will need to provide this information. You will need a solid list of reliable vendors who can perform anything from rekeys, winterizations, lawn service, plumbing, electrical, HVAC repairs, trash outs, painting, carpet cleaning and/or installation, etc. Remember, investing in repairs could over improve an asset for the market in which it is located. Investing in too little repairs could mean the seller is missing the opportunity to attract a strong buyer base.

National Preservation Companies Role

- More and more clients are choosing to outsource the initial services and ongoing maintenance to national preservation companies.
- Refer to your assignment letter to determine who is responsible.
- Communicate with National Preservation Company for specific needs at your property.
- You may be asked to inspect the property after completion of initial services to verify work was completed to your satisfaction.
- Know who to contact at the preservation company for any needed items, emergency repairs, dewinterizations, etc.

Code Violations

- Notify client or preservation company when property is posted with a code violation.
- Code violations are treated very seriously by your client.
- If you are responsible for maintaining the property, you could lose the listing due to code violations incurred after you have taken possession of the property.
- The city may perform snow removal, trash removal, tree trimming, and grass cutting, etc., if the property in not being maintained according to city code standards.

Vacant property registration and city, county, state laws and ordinances

- Vacant property registrations are becoming more prevalent with the increased number of vacant homes.
- Know the rules and regulations for each city in which you have listings. You may be responsible for registering the property, and paying for this. Other times, it will be the national preservation company who is responsible for this.
- You will want to know specific city, county, state laws and ordinances. For example, you will want to know how much snow requires snow removal. You will want to know about zoning and permit requirements. The list goes on and on, and will vary based on your property.

The BPO and how to value REO assets

- The BPO must be completed on time and online. The timeframe for completion of the interior BPO is usually 72 hours after assignment.
- A full set of color photographs with date and time stamp should be submitted.
- Indicate value: "as is", "repaired" or 30 to 90 day value.

- In the comments section, be thorough and complete in describing the market, employment, trends and marketing strategy.
- The interior BPO is the foundation by which pricing is determined.
- Your client will request a full appraisal or a secondary BPO, as well. They will compare this report to yours and make their pricing decision.
- BPOs have been covered in the prior section. Your accuracy in pricing properties is key for repeat business.
- Know your clients expectations. Are they looking for a 30 day, 60 day or 90 day sale? Are they looking for an "as-is" sale, investor sale, FHA buyer, etc?
- Make sure you understand the role that repairs play in the valuation process. Do not suggest repairs over and above what is customary for the neighborhood, or to put the asset in average condition.
- The potential market value will determine the amount of repairs needed.
- As always the REO broker will make recommendations for repairs needed to get the maximum sales price, however the client will always make the final decision.

How to handle HOA rules, regulations and payments

- Each client will have different expectations. Some will require you to only list the HOA contact information. Others will require you to get an itemized statement of any past due balance and provide to the client. Other clients may require you to not only get the itemized statement, pay for the requested documents, pay monthly HOA dues ongoing until close and submit for reimbursement.
- Do not obligate the seller to provide HOA documents over and above what is provided by the title company. They will not typically pay for this. You will want to disclose this as a buyer cost.
- Make sure you are maintaining the property according to the guidelines in an HOA community. This could mean you may need to increase lawn maintenance, turn on water and sprinkler systems, etc. Some HOA's will not allow the posting of real estate signs in the yard. Others will not allow boarded up windows. Don't get caught with your property being cited for HOA violations.

Utilities

- As the listing broker, you will be responsible for activating gas, electric and water. You are responsible for any required deposits. These deposits are not reimbursable.
- You will be required to get an itemized print out of past due water charges. This will need to be paid for, and then submitted for reimbursement. Again, refer to your listing guidelines.
- National preservation companies may be charged with activating utilities, however you may be required to provide the correct information to them. You may need to follow up to make sure service was transferred. For example, if a past due water bill is not paid, you may not be able to get water turned on for an inspection.
- For properties with well and septic, you will need to research well permit information to provide to a buyer.

- Upon closing, you will be required to call each utility company to terminate service. Your clients will not pay for service beyond the close date.

How to submit invoices for reimbursement

- Every company will have specific guidelines/format.
- Some will have you submit invoices for reimbursement on their own website; others will use other portals or invoicing sites.
- You will be required to submit a W-9.
- The expectation is that the broker will pay for most expenses and then submit for reimbursement.
- You will need to submit an original or copy of original invoice, a copy of your check for services as proof of payment, within 30 days of service date.
- If payment is to be made to a different vendor due to scope of work or high expense, you will need up front approval. The vendor must submit a W-9 and be willing to wait 30 – 90 days for reimbursement.
- Honesty is required. Vendors used must not be related to you. You may not have a side company that performs the work. You will be required to use bonded and insured vendors. Never pad a bill.
- Photos of all before and after repair work must be provided prior to receiving any reimbursement. Some companies even require before and after photos of lawn care and snow removal.
- Pay very careful attention to billing. The fastest way to go out of business is to not submit your invoices for reimbursement on a timely basis.

Maintaining Properties

- The REO broker is solely responsible for the ongoing maintenance of the property unless a national preservation company has been hired to do this.
- Most companies require you to visit the property once per week to make sure the property is maintained and still secured.
- Post your contact information on every property in addition to your listing sign.
- The preservation or integrity of the asset is the job of the REO broker.
- Complete an interior inspection on every visit to make sure the heat is set properly, there is no water damage, to pick up trash, newspapers, flyers, etc.
- Make sure the property has not been posted with a code violation.
- Make sure all access points are properly secured.

The REO Listing Agreement

- Read the listing agreement, and then read it again.
- The listing agreement will outline the sales price, listing period, commission paid, referral fee if any and any and all pertinent information.

Income=REO Simplified, Presented by James A. Browning

- You will have 24 – 48 hours to get the property listed in the MLS, and submit the signed listing agreement, and a copy of the MLS. The MLS should have a photo of the property, with your sign displayed.
- Add as many photos as possible to the MLS.
- You may be required to submit your property to other websites, as required by your client.
- You may be required to get certain repairs done.
- Understand all paperwork and documents from the initial assignment to the closing of the asset or for the duration of the listing contract.
- Provide specific directions on how to access the property.
- Provide specific information in the MLS such as "sold as is", buyer responsible for de/rewinterization, buyer to verify all measurements, HOA, buyer responsible for HOA documents, etc.
- Determine your marketing strategy.

Marketing Strategies – "As Is" sale

- The REO broker is solely responsible for the marketing of the property.
- The marketing of the REO property is very different than a normal retail listing.
- The listing will need to be placed on REO websites.
- Most clients require the listing agent to hold open houses year round, and to advertise in their local market. Any costs associated with this are not reimbursable.
- Be creative in finding ways to get your property sold.
- Upscale and higher end listings may require different strategies.
- Place marketing materials within each home.
- Partner with lenders or utilize your clients lending partners.
- The property is being sold, "as is, where is".

How to Process REO Offers

- All clients will require buyers to provide a full lender pre-approval letter. Make sure you understand what your client requires in a lender letter.
- Cash offers will require proof of cash funds in the form of a recent bank statement or letter from a bank.
- Financed offers with significant down payment will require both lender letter and proof of cash funds.
- Both lender pre-approvals and proof of funds can not be more than 30 – 60 days old, depending on your clients' requirements.
- Both the lender letter and proof of funds must have a company representative's signature and contact information.
- If a property will not go FHA, fully disclose this in MLS as to what terms the bank will accept.
- Know how to get offers accepted.
- Prep selling brokers. Most banks will not pay for a survey or ILC. Others will only allow certain items for buyers closing costs. Some clients will not pay for the seller

paid title insurance policy. Assignable contracts are almost always automatically rejected. Most banks will select the Title Company; this is a non-negotiable item.

- Know whether your seller will require certified funds for earnest money deposit.
- Know exactly what the bank will require – state contract, bank addendum, etc.
- Present all offers.
- In multiple offer situations, request highest and best right up front.
- Allow a minimum of 72 hours for the seller to provisionally accept the offer.
- All offers are subject to final client and investor approval.

An offer has been accepted, now what?

- Adhere to client timelines when returning contract to client. Most require contract, bank addendum, lender letter or proof of funds, copy of earnest money check, and any and all state disclosures in one PDF file.
- LLC or Corporate buyers are required to provide Certificate of Good Standing documents as well as Articles of Incorporation showing who the authorized signers are.
- Pay attention to your clients' inspection requirements. Some allow for an inspection after contract is ratified, others require inspections right up front.
- Do not allow buyers to make changes to bank addenda language. This will void the contract and require you to resubmit all documents.

Managing under contact properties through closing

- Provide selling agent and title company (if applicable) a copy of the fully executed contract.
- Make sure earnest money is deposited and you have a receipt. Some clients require you to provide them with a copy.
- Follow all addendum dates. The Addendum supersedes the state contract. Pay careful attention to inspection and financing deadlines.
- Make sure water is on if required for buyers' inspection.
- Coordinate dewinterization if appropriate.
- Communicate with selling broker, lender and title company.
- Make sure you communicate with the asset manager regarding any delays, inspection items, lending issues, etc. They all have their own quotas to meet each month and do not like being surprised at the last minute with contract amendments, extensions or terminations.
- Make sure the selling agent and buyer understand the term, sold "as is".
- Be proactive in overcoming issues and concerns. Asset Managers rely on your expertise to find a way to get their properties sold.
- Should an extension be required, make sure the selling agent and buyer are aware of any bank required per diem penalties.
- Prepare selling agent for possible closing delays due to a delay in the recording of vesting deed.
- Most clients require anywhere from 48 -96 hours to turn around a seller signed HUD. This means lender figures need to be into the closing agent 4 days in advance of close if

you want a seller signed HUD at closing. Buyers cannot take possession of the property without a seller signed HUD and transfer of funds.

- Continue to monitor the property until the day of close. Buyers are not allowed to begin repairs. Notify the asset manager should the condition of the property change in any way.
- Make sure buyers understand the need to rekey property immediately upon taking possession, and that all utilities are cancelled the day of closing.
- Communication can't be stressed enough. You want to make sure your property closes on time!
- Monthly marketing reports and updated BPOs are still requested for properties that are under contract. All assets need to continually be re-evaluated.

Monthly Marketing Reports

These reports are usually due between the 1st and 5th of each month or every 30 days from list date. These cannot be late. You run the risk of having the listing pulled by not meeting these deadlines. In addition, updated BPOs are usually requested every 60- 90 days.

Both the monthly marketing report and BPO are your opportunity to update your client on the number of showings, offers, open houses, advertising placements, positive and negative showing comments, new price recommendation and anything else of importance regarding the subject property. This is your chance to let them know of changes in the market, update them with new solds and listings in the area, and tell them what needs to be done to get the property sold in the next 30 -60 days. Some clients will have automatic price reductions; others will rely very heavily on your reports to determine if there should be a price reduction.

Understanding Risk Management and Liability

To protect both yourself and the client, make sure you understand proper risk management and liability. The first step is to make sure your company has the proper policies and procedures in place. Follow Fair Housing Laws, avoid anti-trust issues, and follow all RESPA rules. Below is a checklist of guidelines to follow regarding risk management.

- E & O Insurance
- Current knowledge of Federal, State, and local laws
- Recommend inspections
- Maintain detailed notes of communications with all parties
- Maintain detailed notes and photo documentation of all assets
- Follow EPA guidelines with regards to all hazardous conditions
- Document your source of information
- Provide a copy of all required documents to all parties
- Maintain and preserve your clients assets to their guidelines
- Follow all MLS rules and guidelines
- Always use non subjective language in your BPOs, MLS remarks, advertising, etc.

How REO Brokers are evaluated and scored

Ultimately the key to building your REO business is based on your performance and your ability to achieve results. Do well on your initial assignments and you will have a foundation on which to build an expanded client base. Banks and outsourcers are not at all hesitant about finding new agents if you are non responsive, miss deadlines, not proactive, inaccurate in your pricing, have too many contract terminations, do not maintain their properties to their expectations, have code violations, or can't get properties sold within 90 – 120 days. Therefore, treat each and every assignment with the same sense of professionalism, urgency, accountability, and initiative; whether it is a $20,000 listing or a $1,000,000 listing. Almost every bank and outsourcer has some kind of evaluation and scoring process. Listed below are the key factors on which you will be graded:

- Adherence to all guidelines and deadlines, from initial occupancy check through close
- BPO accuracy
- Completion of monthly marketing reports
- Communication
- Ability to get properties sold within 30 – 60 days
- Actual sale price to suggested sale price
- Accuracy in submitting invoices
- High contract to close rate

Remember, you are hired to be the "eyes and ears" for the bank and agree to manage, market and sell properties on their behalf. Before you get started in the REO world, make sure you completely understand both the BPO and REO process. Get as much education as you can, and be prepared to do many BPOs before you receive your first REO listing.

Front view, if snow removal needed, report the need

If property is unsafe, report conditions

Foundation issues, take photos/notes, report conditions

Report unsafe conditions, take photos & document

Needs demolition, take photos/notes, report conditions

Furnace/hotwater heater, take photos & detailed note

Foundation problems, report problems if any

Foundation issues, recommend an inspection

Note landscaping issues, take photos & notes

REO property, note address verification, take photo

Exterior damage, take photos & notes, report

Exterior damage, take photos & notes, report

BPO property, take 3-4 front pictures

Unsafe exterior conditions, take photo & document

Exterior graffiti, take photo & document, report

BPO requests/REO properties come in many forms

Townhomes/Condos, take photos/notes of common areas

Loft projects, possible BPO or REO properties

Bathroom problems, repairs?, report conditions

02.04.2011 12:20

If required to post, post per guidelines

BPO & REO Simplified, Presented by James A. Browning

Secure & board up windows, take photo & document

Report damage and leaks, take photo & document

BPO & REO Simplified, Presented by James A. Browning

Report personal property &/or trash, take photo & document

Report possible water damage, take photo & document

Take detailed notes, & photos, trashout required

Kitchen after trashout & cleaning on REO property

REO listing, good condition

Report missing appliances, take photo & document

Garage trash, take photo & detailed notes

Exterior trash, take photo & document

Front view, take 3-4 photos of front

Burnt grass, take photos and document

Family room trash, take photo & document

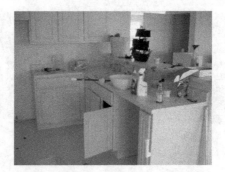

Kitchen condition, check for water leaks/possible repairs

Basement personal property, take photo& document

Backyard, take (3-5) photos from different angles

Sold Comp #1 – 1260 Simpson Ave

Address	1260 Simpson Ave
Proximity to Subject	.08 miles
Sold Price	$175,000
Concessions	$3,000 Slr Pd Closing Costs
Sold Date/Days On Market	Sold 8 days ago, 178 DOM
Location	Suburban
Lot Size	4,000 SF
View	Street, None
Design	Ranch
Square Feet	980
Age	47
Condition	Good
Bedrooms	3
Baths	2
Basement	None
Heating/Cooling	GFA, None
Garage/Carport	1 Car Attached Garage
Porch,Patio,Fireplace,etc.	2 Fireplaces
Fence,Pool,etc.	Fence

Adjustment Worksheet

Feature	Subj	-	Comp	=	Difference	x	Feature Value	=	$ Adjustment
YOC	45	-	47	=	2	x	500	=	$ + 1,000
Bdrm	3	-	3	=	0	x		=	$
Bath	2	-	2	=	0	x		=	$
HVAC	AC	-	None	=	1	x	1,500	=	$ + 1,500
Garage	1	-	1	=	0	x		=	$
Fireplace	1	-	2	=	1	x	1,000	=	$ - 1,000

Total Adjustment $ +1,500

Sold Price - Concessions +/- Adjustment = $173,500
$175,000 – 3,000 + 1,500 = $173,500

Inferior ☐ Superior ☐ Equal ☐

Sold Comp #2 – 1399 Lemont Ave

Address	1399 Lemont Ave
Proximity to Subject	.28 miles
Sold Price	$163,000
Concessions	$0
Sold Date/Days On Market	Sold 183 days ago, 240 DOM
Location	Suburban
Lot Size	3,200 SF
View	Mountains
Design	Ranch
Square Feet	1,020
Age	55
Condition	Good
Bedrooms	3
Baths	2
Basement	None
Heating/Cooling	GFA, Evap Cooler
Garage/Carport	2 Car Attached Garage
Porch,Patio,Fireplace,etc.	1 Fireplace
Fence,Pool,etc.	Fence

Adjustment Worksheet

Feature	Subj	-	Comp	=	Difference	x	Feature Value	=	$ Adjustment
YOC	45	-	55	=	10	x	500	=	$ + 5,000
Bdrm	3	-	3	=	0	x		=	$
Bath	2	-	2	=	0	x		=	$
HVAC	AC	-	Evap	=	1	x	500	=	$ + 500
Garage	1	-	2	=	1	x	3,000	=	$ - 3,000
Fireplace	1	-	1	=	0	x		=	$

Total Adjustment $ + 2,500

Sold Price - Concessions +/- Adjustment = $165,500
$163,000 – 0 + 2,500 = $165,500

Inferior ☐ Superior ☐ Equal ☐

Sold Comp #3 – 1345 Black Hawk St.

Address	1345 Black Hawk St
Proximity to Subject	1.23 miles
Sold Price	$167,000
Concessions	$2,100 Slr Pd Closing Costs
Sold Date/Days On Market	Sold 89 days ago, 120 DOM
Location	Suburban
Lot Size	3,115 SF
View	Street, None
Design	Ranch
Square Feet	1,035
Age	37
Condition	Good
Bedrooms	4
Baths	3
Basement	None
Heating/Cooling	GFA, None
Garage/Carport	1 Car Attached Garage
Porch,Patio,Fireplace,etc.	1 Fireplace
Fence,Pool,etc.	Fence

Adjustment Worksheet

Feature	Subj	-	Comp	=	Difference	x	Feature Value	=	$ Adjustment
YOC	45	-	37	=	8	x	500	=	$ - 4,000
Bdrm	3	-	4	=	1	x	2,000	=	$ - 2,000
Bath	2	-	3	=	1	x	1,500	=	$ - 1,500
HVAC	AC	-	None	=	1	x	1,500	=	$ + 1,500
Garage	1	-	1	=	0	x		=	$
Fireplace	1	-	1	=	0	x		=	$

Total Adjustment $ - 6,000

Sold Price - Concessions +/- Adjustment = $158,900
167,000 – 2,100 – 6,000 = 158,900

Inferior ☐ Superior ☐ Equal ☐

List Comp #1 – 1299 Forest Way

Address	1299 Forest Way
Proximity to Subject	1.2 miles
List Price	$179,900
Concessions	None
Days On Market	15 DOM
Location	Suburban
Lot Size	3,144 SF
View	Street, None
Design	Two Story
Square Feet	1,050
Age	40
Condition	Good
Bedrooms	3
Baths	2
Basement	None
Heating/Cooling	GFA, Evap Cooler
Garage/Carport	2 Car Attached Garage
Porch,Patio,Fireplace,etc.	1 Fireplace
Fence,Pool,etc.	Fence

Adjustment Worksheet

Feature	Subj	-	Comp	=	Difference	x	Feature Value	=	$ Adjustment
YOC	45	-	40	=	5	x	500	=	$ - 2,500
Bdrm	3	-	3	=	0	x		=	$
Bath	2	-	2	=	0	x		=	$
HVAC	AC	-	Evap	=	1	x	500	=	$ +500
Garage	1	-	2	=	1	x	3,000	=	$ - 3,000
Fireplace	1	-	1	=	0	x		=	$

Total Adjustment $ - 5,000

List Price - Concessions +/- Adjustment = $174,900
179,900 – 0 – 5,000 = 174,900

Inferior □ Superior □ Equal □

List Comp #2 – 1278 Walters Ave

Address	1278 Walters Ave
Proximity to Subject	.67 miles
List Price	$163,000
Concessions	None
Days On Market	185 DOM
Location	Suburban
Lot Size	3,200 SF
View	Street, None
Design	Ranch
Square Feet	1,095
Age	45
Condition	Good
Bedrooms	4
Baths	2
Basement	None
Heating/Cooling	GFA, None
Garage	None
Porch,Patio,Fireplace,etc.	None
Fence,Pool,etc.	Fence

Adjustment Worksheet

Feature	Subj	-	Comp	=	Difference	x	Feature Value	=	$ Adjustment
YOC	45	-	45	=	0	x		=	$
Bdrm	3	-	4	=	1	x	2,000	=	$ - 2,000
Bath	2	-	2	=	0	x		=	$
HVAC	AC	-	None	=	1	x	1,500	=	$ + 1,500
Garage	1	-	0	=	1	x	3,000	=	$ + 3,000
Fireplace	1	-	0	=	1	x	1,000	=	$ + 1,000

Total Adjustment $ +3,500

List Price - Concessions +/- Adjustment = $166,500
163,000 + 3,500 = 166,500

Inferior ☐ Superior ☐ Equal ☐

BPO & REO Simplified, Presented by James A. Browning

List Comp #3 – 2381 74th Pl.

Address	2381 74th Pl.
Proximity to Subject	.09 miles
List Price	$137,900
Concessions	None
Days On Market	56 DOM
Location	Suburban
Lot Size	2,890 SF
View	Street, None
Design	Ranch
Square Feet	975
Age	58
Condition	Fair
Bedrooms	2
Baths	2
Basement	None
Heating/Cooling	GFA, AC
Garage	1 Car Garage
Porch,Patio,Fireplace,etc.	None
Fence,Pool,etc.	Fence

Adjustment Worksheet

Feature	Subj	-	Comp	=	Difference	x	Feature Value	=	$ Adjustment
YOC	45	-	58	=	13	x	500	=	$ + 6,500
Bdrm	3	-	2	=	1	x	2,000	=	$ + 2,000
Bath	2	-	2	=	0	x		=	$
HVAC	AC	-	AC	=	0	x		=	$
Garage	1	-	1	=	0	x		=	$
Fireplace	1	-	0	=	1	x	1,000	=	$ + 1,000

Total Adjustment $ + 9,500

List Price - Concessions +/- Adjustment = $147,400
137,900 + 9,500 = 147,400

Inferior □ Superior □ Equal □